Mommy Loves You Exactly as You Are!

Mommy Loves You Exactly as You Are!

Helping Children Know How Much They Are Loved and How Loveable They Are

By Wade Galt

Possibility Infinity Publishing

ISBN   978-1-934108-05-5

Reinvesting in Our Children

25% of the profit from the sale of this book
goes to organizations and charities that seek to spread love,
teach parents to love their children, and prevent and heal
the effects of child abuse.

To Francisco & Luna…

Our Beautiful Children & Bundles of Joy.

Thank You for Blessing Our Lives with Your Love, Laughter, Hugs, Kisses, Smiles (and the Other Stuff, too) and for Helping Us Experience What It Means for a Parent to Truly Love Their Children.

To God…

Thank You for Francisco & Luna and for Each Other.

To Parents & Children Everywhere…

May You Experience What It Is for a Parent to Truly Love Their Child and a Child to Feel and Know They are Fully Loved Exactly as They Are.

Love:

I Accept You...

As You Are...

No Matter What.

Remembering and Maintaining the Love

Babies are so easy to love. It feels so natural to love a newborn child unconditionally. The love just naturally flows out of us. Nobody has to teach us. Nobody has to ask us. Nobody has to convince us. It just happens.

Somewhere between the first diaper and the first day of school, we can begin to lose our sense of awe about our children. The things we used to find so cute may not be so entertaining any more. We might find ourselves losing patience with the same "angel" we held just moments ago.

How wonderful it would be if we could always love, cherish, and appreciate our children as gorgeous, loving, angels. How great it would be to carry our love with us and maintain it powerfully forever.

We can do that. We simply need to be nudged to remember. We just need to be reminded what we hold dear and precious. We only need to take time out for a few moments and bask in the memory (and the present moment reality) of what is so amazingly and divinely wonderful about our gifts from the divine.

This book is one of those reminders.

My hope is that this book helps you…

1) Let your child or children know how special they are.

2) Remember how special your child or children are.

3) Understand how much your parents love(d) you, whether or not they ever shared this with you.

Enjoy!

Mommy Loves You Exactly as You Are!

I Was So Excited to Meet You Before You Were Even Born!

I Was as Happy as I Could Be When You Finally Arrived!

And I am Just as Happy as Ever That You Are In My Life!

I Love You Exactly as You Are!

You Don't Have to Do Anything for Me to Love You!

I Know You Do Your

Best!

I Love You Exactly as You Are!

You Don't Have to Say Anything for Me to Love You!

I Love You No Matter What You Say or What You Don't Say!

I Love You Exactly as You Are!

You Don't Have to Know Anything for Me to Love You!

If You Never Passed a Single Test or Read a Single Book, I Would Still Love You!

I Will Teach You Many Things In Life, But It's Most Important For You to Know and Remember How Much I Love You!

I Love You Exactly as You Are!

You Don't Have to Be or Do Anything for Me to Love You!

You Are Perfectly Loveable

Just the Way You Are!

You Are Completely Loved Even If You Never Do Anything Else In Your Life!

I Love You Exactly as You Are!

You Don't Have to Be Like Me for Me to Love You!

You Don't Have to Like

What I Like!

You Don't Have to Think

What I Think!

You Don't Have to Believe What I Believe!

You Are Your Own Person, and You Are Wonderful Just the Way You Are!

You Will Not Always Agree with Me, and That's Okay!

You Can Make Your Own
Choices and Know That I
Will Still Be Here to Love
You and Accept You
Exactly As You Are!

I Love You Exactly as You Are!

You Don't Have to Always Obey Me for Me to Love You!

I Will Not Stop Loving You Just Because You Do Not Listen to Me!

I May Not Let You Do Certain Things, And I May Take Privileges Away From You, But That Doesn't Mean I Don't Love You!

I Didn't Always Do What My Parent(s) Said, and That's Okay, Too!

I Love You Exactly as You Are!

You Don't Have to Wear

the Same Clothes I Wear!

I Know You Will Find a Style of Your Own, and It Will Be Beautiful, Just Like You!

I Love You Exactly as You Are!

You Don't Have to Play the Same Sports or Games that I Played!

Even If You Never Played a Game In Your Life, I Would Still Love You!

A Game Is Just a Game, But You Are My Angel!

You Are Much More Important to Me than Any Game!

I Love You Exactly as You Are!

You Don't Have to Always Get Good Grades for Me to Love You!

Good Grades are Nice, But You are Much More Important Than Good Grades!

I Still Want to You to Work Hard and Get Good Grades, and I Will Do Whatever I Can Do to Help You!

But It Is More Important That You Know How Much I Love You!

Good Grades or Not, You Will Always Be My Precious Child!

I Love You Exactly as You Are!

You Don't Have to Do What I Do for a Living for Me to Love You!

I Know That You Have

Dreams, Too!

You May Want to Be a

Firefighter, a Teacher, a

Business Person, or a

Million Other Things!

If You Want to Do What I Do for A Living, That's Great!

I Will Love You and Support You and Do Everything Else I Can to Help You!

If You Don't Want to Do What I Do for A Living, That's Great, Too!

I Will Love You and Support You and Do Everything Else I Can to Help You!

I Love You Exactly as You Are!

You Don't Have to Always Be Kind and Loving for Me to Love You!

I Hope You Are Kind and Loving to Me, But I Know You Will Have Days When You Are Not!

I Have Plenty of Love to Give to You When You Feel You Don't Have Enough!

I Love You Exactly as You Are!

More Than Anything, I Want You to Know How Much I Love You!

I Want You to Be Happy and Have a Wonderful Life!

I Also Want to Help You to Be Happy and Have a Wonderful Life!

Most of the Times, I Will Be Able to Help You!

Sometimes, Even Though I Love You, I Will Get in Your Way as You Look to Create What You Most Want in Life!

I Won't Mean to Do This,

But I'm Human, Too!

Just Know That No

Matter What...

No Matter What...

I Will Always Love You...

Exactly As You Are!

Always!

Acknowledgments

Thank you God for loving me so much and allowing me to know how loved I am.

Thank you Mom and Dad for loving me so much and being such a great role model for me.

Thank you Rossana for being such a great wife and mother and making it so easy for me to stay in touch with the most loving side of myself.

Thank you Natalie and Brad for being such a great example of people who love their children so much.

Thank you Christian for showing up in my life and allowing me to practice being a loving parent from a young age.

Thank you Pablo and Pilar for loving Rossana so much and raising such a loving daughter. I am truly blessed.

About the Author

Wade has led retreats and personal growth workshops, authored books on spirituality, personal growth, finance, parenting, business growth & more.

He has worked successfully as a life coach, 4-day work week mentor, organizational consultant, computer trainer, sales consultant, executive coach, speaker, mental health counselor, management consultant, software designer and programmer, author, business analyst, financial counselor, and in many other capacities.

Wade has a Bachelor's degree in Marketing and a Master's degree in Mental Health Counseling Psychology.

He lives happily with his wife and children.

His email address is wade@wadegalt.com .

Author Blog & Website

You may visit Wade's blog & website at www.wadegalt.com .

Other Helpful Reading *

Guess How Much I Love You by Sam Mcbratney and Anita Jeram

I Love You More by Laura Duksta, Karen Keesler

The Parent's Tao Te Ching: Ancient Advice for Modern Parents: A New Interpretation by William C. Martin

The Seven Spiritual Laws for Parents: Guiding Your Children to Success and Fulfillment by Deepak Chopra

Incredible You!: 10 Ways to Be Happy Inside and Out by Wayne W. Dyer

* The author does not agree with every opinion and point of view presented in every book; however, these books have been a great source of inspiration for the author.

25% of the profit from the sale of this book goes to organizations and charities that seek to spread love, teach parents to love their children, and prevent and heal the effects of child abuse.

.

Mommy Loves You Exactly as You Are!

Also by Wade Galt

Put Your Money Where Your Soul Is

A Simple Guide to Spending Your
Money, Time and Life Purposefully

Learn how to free up additional time, money and energy by redefining your relationships with money, time, people, and things.

Simple strategies, exercises & tools help you make powerful changes with very little effort or struggle.

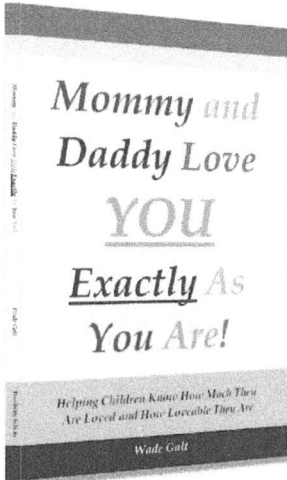

Mommy and Daddy Love You Exactly As You Are!

Helping Children Know How Much They
Are Loved and How Loveable They Are

My hope is that this book helps you...

1) Let your child or children know how special they are.

2) Remember how special your child or children are.

3) Understand how much your parents love(d) you, whether or not they ever shared this with you.

Mommy Loves You Exactly As You Are!

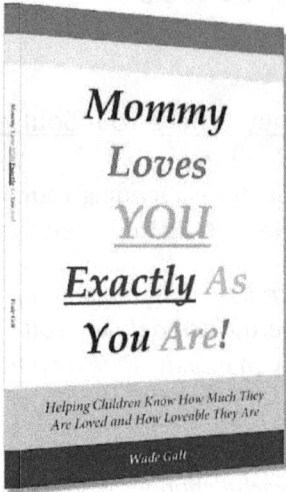

Helping Children Know How Much They Are Loved and How Loveable They Are

My hope is that this book helps you...

1) Let your child or children know how special they are.

2) Remember how special your child or children are.

3) Understand how much your parents love(d) you, whether or not they ever shared this with you.

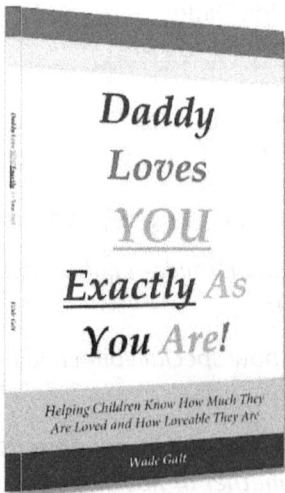

Daddy Loves You Exactly As You Are!

Helping Children Know How Much They Are Loved and How Loveable They Are

My hope is that this book helps you...

1) Let your child or children know how special they are.

2) Remember how special your child or children are.

3) Understand how much your parents love(d) you, whether or not they ever shared this with you.

The *God Equals Love* Book Series

(Free eBook Versions Available for All Books)

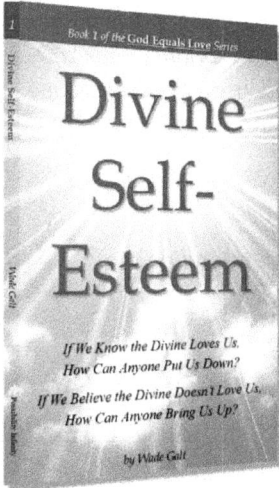

Book 1 - Divine Self-Esteem

Learning to Love Ourselves
the Way the Divine Loves Us

If we know the Divine loves us, how can anyone put us down?

If we believe the Divine doesn't love us, how can anyone bring us up?

Learn to see yourself through divinely loving eyes and catch a glimpse of the divinely-made miracle you are.

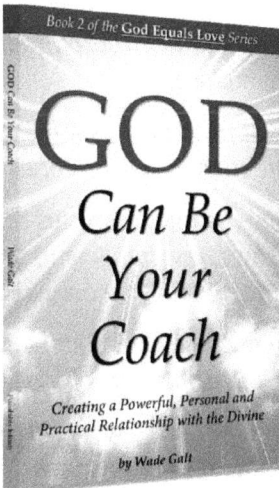

Book 2 - GOD Can Be Your Coach

Creating a Powerful, Personal and
Practical Relationship with the Divine

Create More Joy, Happiness, Love, Peace and Purpose in Your Life.

Learn One Simple Way to form a more powerful connection & relationship.

If You Knew You Could Connect with the Divine Anytime You Choose to Receive Guidance, Support, and Peace, Would You?

Will You?

3 - GOD Loves You Exactly As You Are!

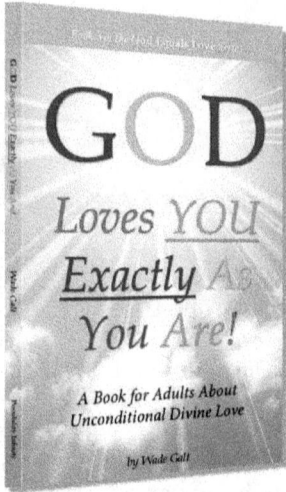

Understanding & Experiencing Unconditional Divine Love

An Invitation to Consider & Experience the Life-Altering Understanding That You are Completely and Unconditionally Loved and Loveable EXACTLY AS YOU ARE!

What If God Loves You EXACTLY as You are?

How Would Understanding that Transform Your Life?

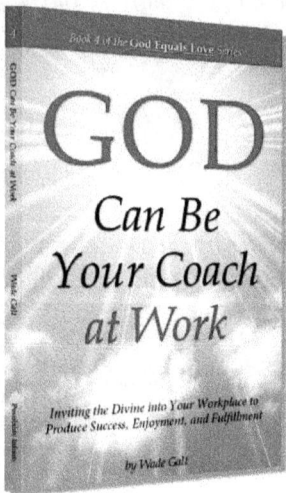

Book 4 - GOD Can Be Your Coach at Work

Inviting the Divine into Your Workplace to Produce Success, Enjoyment & Fulfillment

Few of us fully live our highest spiritual values in our workplace.

This is a source of frustration, shame, guilt & dissatisfaction for billions of us.

What if the divine actually wants us to experience life, love, joy, fulfillment, and abundance inside and outside our work?

What if the divine cares about our work simply because the divine cares for us?

This book is an invitation to work WITH the divine to create divinely inspired results for you and the world.

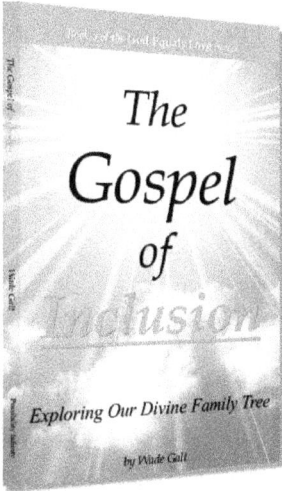

Book 5 - The Gospel of Inclusion

Exploring Our Divine Family Tree

Who is included in God's plan? Is it only people like me? Only people like you? What atrocities & apathy do we justify daily by declaring others are outside of God's chosen circle of people?

What if we really are part of one divine family? What would that mean? How would we have to change?

WARNING! Reading this book may lead you to (1) consider the possibility that we're all God's children and (2) do something about that. Proceed at your own risk!

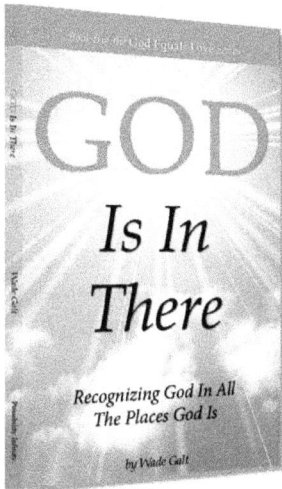

Book 6 - God Is In There

Recognizing God In All The Places God Is

If you could teach only one spiritual lesson, what would you teach?

What truth could you share that is so powerful, it would fundamentally transform the way others live?

There are a few core ideas that most spiritual traditions hold as true. Some believe that the most powerful and life-transforming truths are so self-evident and so obvious that all traditions agree about them.

This book contains one of those ideas.

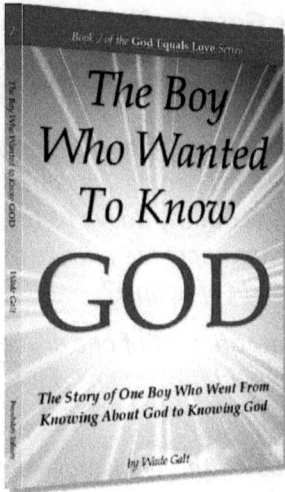

7 - The Boy Who Wanted to Know God

The Story of One Boy Who Went from Knowing About God to Knowing God

What would you be willing to do in order to meet God?

Join a curious and excited young boy on his journey to meeting the divine.

You might meet God, too.

The journey may be shorter and simpler than you think.

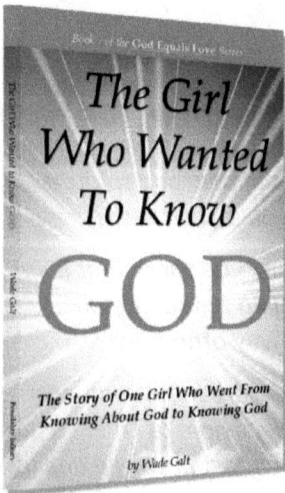

7 - The Girl Who Wanted to Know God

The Story of One Girl Who Went from Knowing About God to Knowing God

What would you be willing to do in order to meet God?

Join a curious and excited young girl on her journey to meeting the divine.

You might meet God, too.

The journey may be shorter and simpler than you think.

Translated into Spanish (More to Come)

Autoestima Divina

Aprendiendo a Amarnos De la Forma en que Dios nos Ama

Si sabemos que el Divino nos ama, ¿cómo podemos sentirnos mal con nosotros mismos?

Si creemos que el Divino no nos ama, ¿cómo podemos sentirnos bien con nosotros mismos?

Aprender a verse a sí mismo a través de los ojos de amor de Dios y echar un vistazo a el milagro hecho de Dios-que eres.

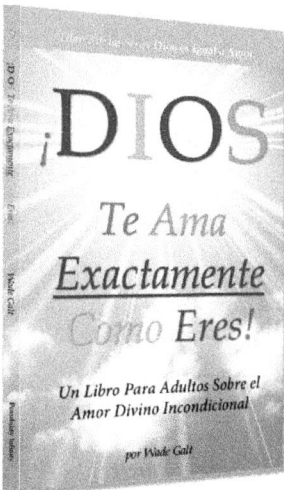

DIOS Te Ama Exactamente Como Eres

Un Libro Para Adultos Sobre el Amor Divino Incondicional

¿Y Si Dios te ama EXACTAMENTE como eres? ¿De que manera ese entendimiento transformaría tu vida?

Esto Es Una Simple Invitación... Para Considerar y Experimentar... Un Entendimiento de la Vida Alternativo...

Tú Eres Completa e Incondicionalmente... Amado y Adorable... EXACTAMENTE COMO ERES!

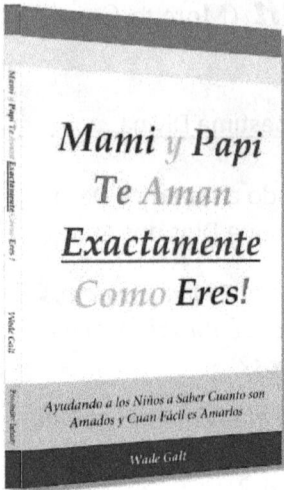

Mami y Papi Te Aman Exactamente Como Eres!

Ayudando a los Niños a Saber Cuanto son Amados y Cuan Fácil es Amarlos

Mi esperanza es que este libro te ayude a...

1) Hacer que tus niños sepan cuan especiales son.

2) Recordarte cuan especiales son tus niños.

3) Comprender cuanto te aman o te amaron tus padres ya sea que compartieran o no esto contigo.

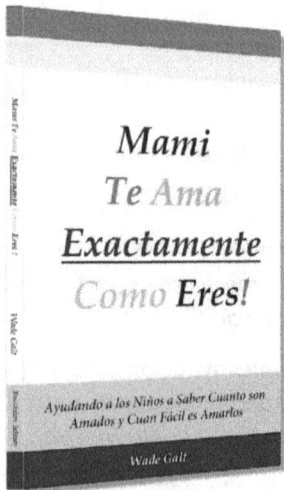

Mami Te Ama Exactamente Como Eres!

Ayudando a los Niños a Saber Cuanto son Amados y Cuan Fácil es Amarlos

Mi esperanza es que este libro te ayude a...

1) Hacer que tus niños sepan cuan especiales son.

2) Recordarte cuan especiales son tus niños.

3) Comprender cuanto te aman o te amaron tus padres ya sea que compartieran o no esto contigo.

Papi Te Ama Exactamente Como Eres!

Papi
Te Ama
Exactamente
Como Eres!

Ayudando a los Niños a Saber Cuanto son
Amados y Cuan Fácil es Amarlos

Mi esperanza es que este libro te ayude a...

1) Hacer que tus niños sepan cuan especiales son.

2) Recordarte cuan especiales son tus niños.

3) Comprender cuanto te aman o te amaron tus padres ya sea que compartieran o no esto contigo.

To see these books and other books not listed here, visit www.wadegalt.com/books .

All profits from the sale of the GOD EQUALS LOVE books go to organizations and charities that seek to end unnecessary hunger and poverty.

New Book & Program Notifications

If you'd like to be emailed when we release new books, audios and other programs please visit www.wadegalt.com/notifiy to sign up for these notifications.

Share the Message & the Love

I hope this helps you see & feel how truly amazing and miraculous of a creation you are and how much the divine values you.

If you found the book to be helpful, would you please be so kind as to write a review on Amazon for the book or share the book on Facebook, Instagram, Twitter or other social media so others may know how it helped you?

Even if it's a super-short review, every little bit helps.

Thank you so much.

If there's anything I can do to help you further with this work, please email me at is <u>wade@wadegalt.com</u> .

All my best,

Wade